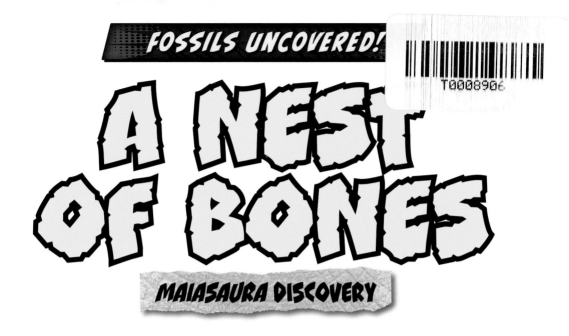

FOSSILS UNCOVERED!

A NEST OF BONES

MAIASAURA DISCOVERY

By Sarah Eason

Illustrated by Ludovic Sallé

BEARPORT
PUBLISHING

Minneapolis, Minnesota

BEAR CLAW

Credits: 20b, © Warpaint/Shutterstock; 21t, © YuRi Photolife/Shutterstock; 21b, © N-sky/Shutterstock; 22l, © Kriengsak Wiriyakrieng/Shutterstock; 22r, © Microgen/Shutterstock; 23b, © LegART/Shutterstock.

Editor: Jennifer Sanderson
Proofreader: Harriet McGregor
Designer: Paul Myerscough
Picture Researcher: Rachel Blount

DISCLAIMER: This graphic story is a dramatization based on true events. It is intended to give the reader a sense of the narrative rather than a presentation of actual details as they occurred.

Library of Congress Cataloging-in-Publication Data

Names: Eason, Sarah, author. | Salle, Ludovic, 1985- illustrator.
Title: A nest of bones : Maiasaura discovery / by Sarah Eason ; illustrated by Ludovic Sallé.
Description: Bear claw books. | Minneapolis, Minnesota : Bearport Publishing Company, [2022] | Series: Fossils uncovered! | Includes index.
Identifiers: LCCN 2021026704 (print) | LCCN 2021026705 (ebook) | ISBN 9781636913353 (library binding) | ISBN 9781636913421 (paperback) | ISBN 9781636913490 (ebook)
Subjects: LCSH: Horner, John R.--Juvenile literature. | Maiasaura--Montana--Juvenile literature. | Maiasaura--Montana--Comic books, strips, etc. | Dinosaur tracks--Montana--Juvenile literature. | Paleontological excavations--Montana--Juvenile literature. | Paleontology--Juvenile literature.
Classification: LCC QE862.O65 E27 2022 (print) | LCC QE862.O65 (ebook) | DDC 567.914--dc23
LC record available at https://lccn.loc.gov/2021026704
LC ebook record available at https://lccn.loc.gov/2021026705

For more information, write to Bearport Publishing, 5357 Penn Avenue South, Minneapolis, MN 55419. Printed in the United States of America.

CONTENTS

CHAPTER 1

A ROCK SHOP SURPRISE

In 1978, Jack Horner was visiting a rock and **fossil** shop in Montana. As a fossil hunter, he was constantly looking for something new and exciting.

HI, MARION. I HEARD YOU FOUND SOME INTERESTING FOSSILS.

SURE DID. TAKE A LOOK.

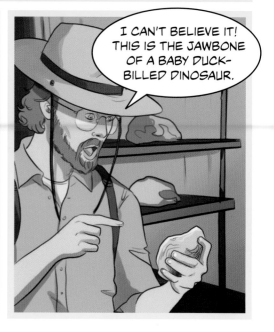

I CAN'T BELIEVE IT! THIS IS THE JAWBONE OF A BABY DUCK-BILLED DINOSAUR.

4

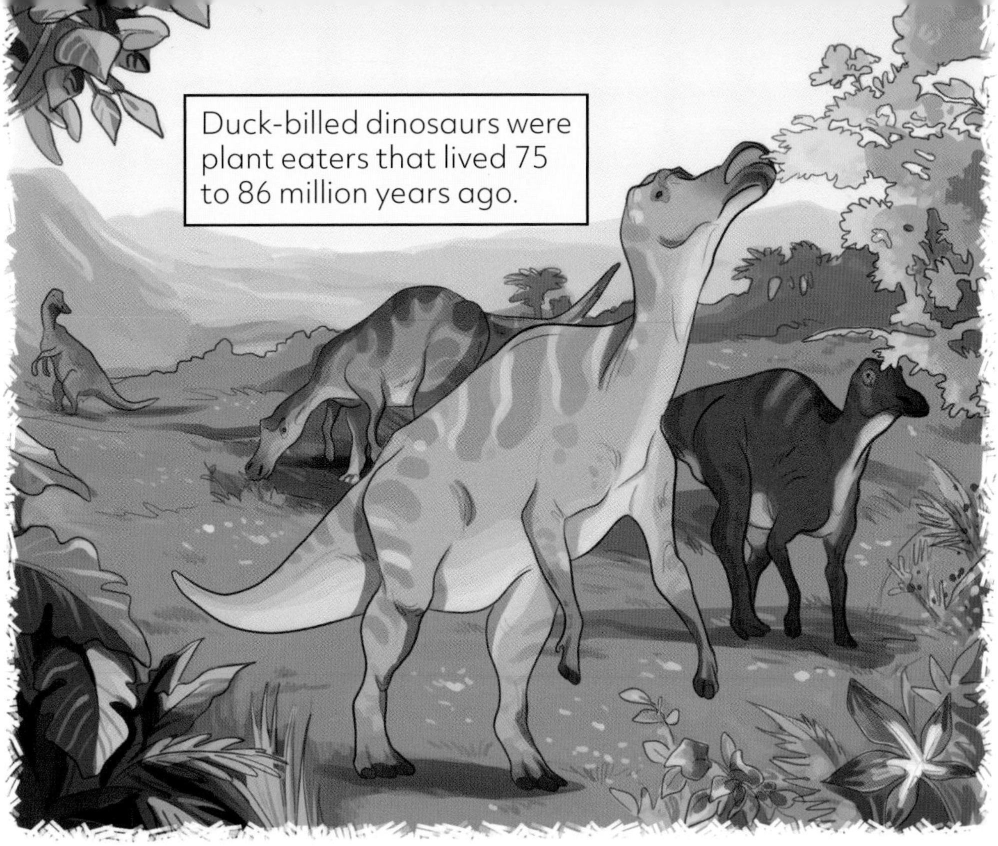
Duck-billed dinosaurs were plant eaters that lived 75 to 86 million years ago.

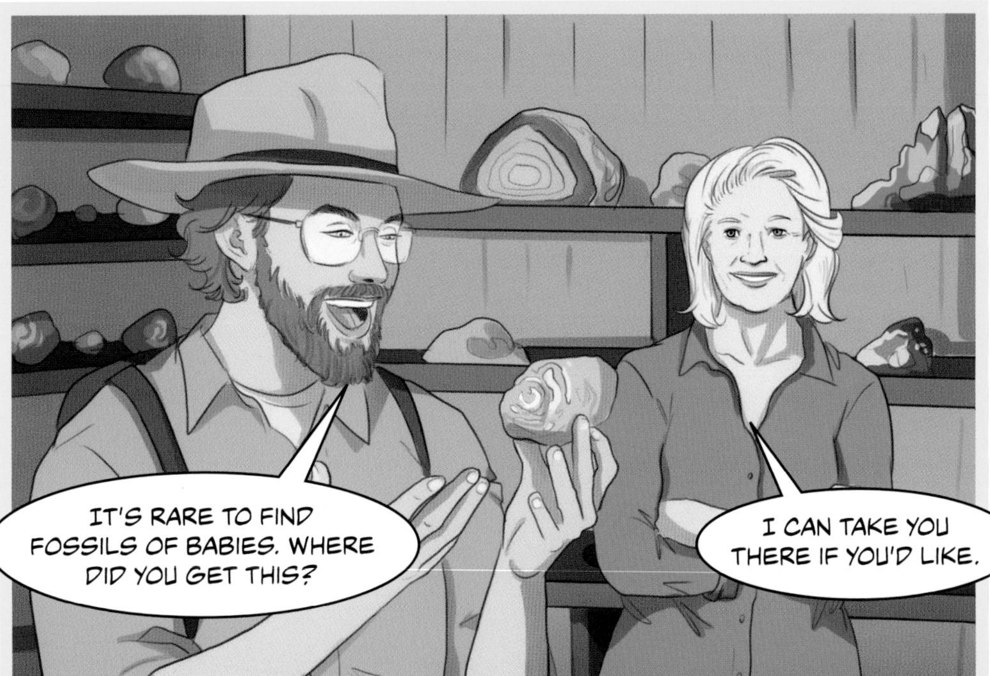
IT'S RARE TO FIND FOSSILS OF BABIES. WHERE DID YOU GET THIS?
I CAN TAKE YOU THERE IF YOU'D LIKE.

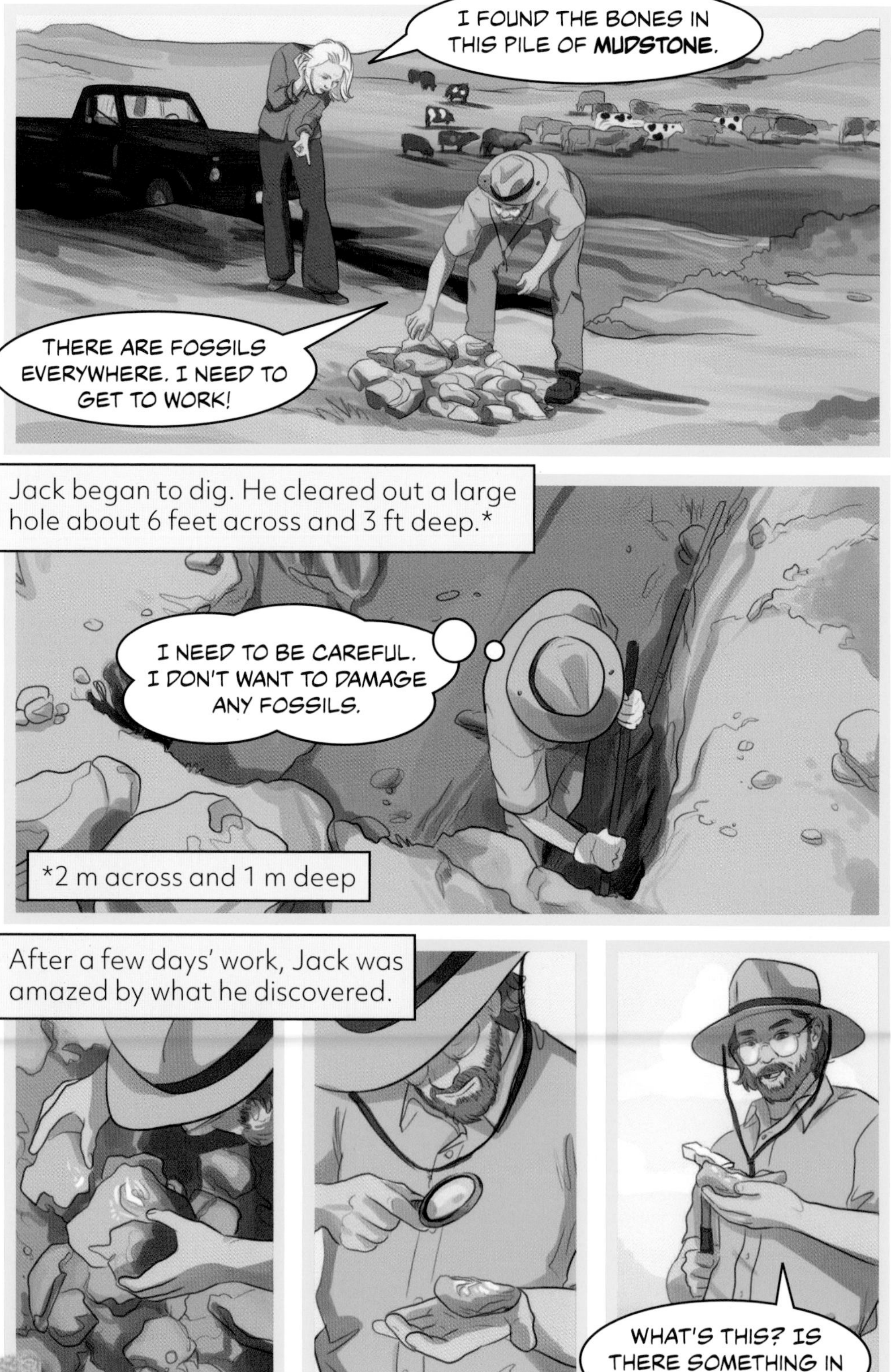
I FOUND THE BONES IN THIS PILE OF **MUDSTONE**.
THERE ARE FOSSILS EVERYWHERE. I NEED TO GET TO WORK!
Jack began to dig. He cleared out a large hole about 6 feet across and 3 ft deep.*
I NEED TO BE CAREFUL. I DON'T WANT TO DAMAGE ANY FOSSILS.
*2 m across and 1 m deep
After a few days' work, Jack was amazed by what he discovered.
WHAT'S THIS? IS THERE SOMETHING IN THIS MUDSTONE?

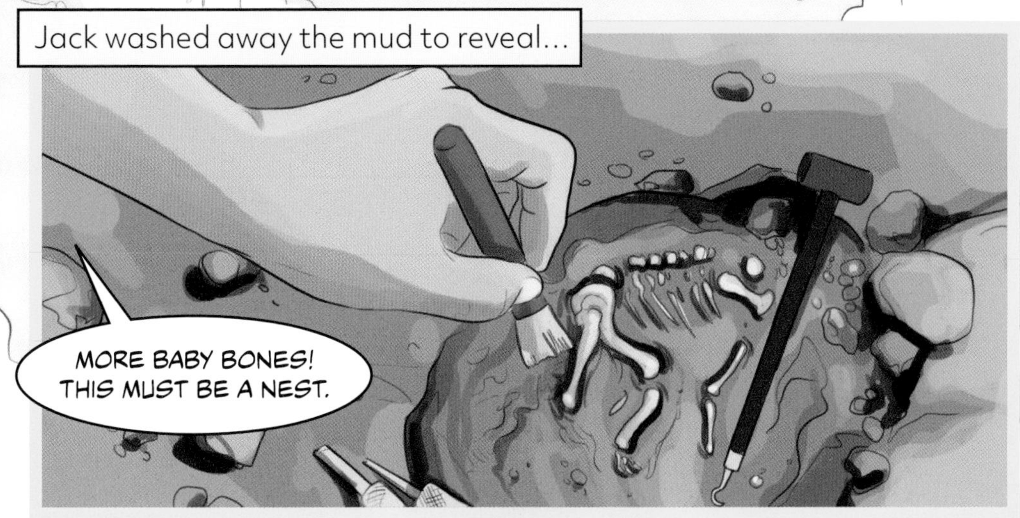
Jack washed away the mud to reveal...
MORE BABY BONES! THIS MUST BE A NEST.

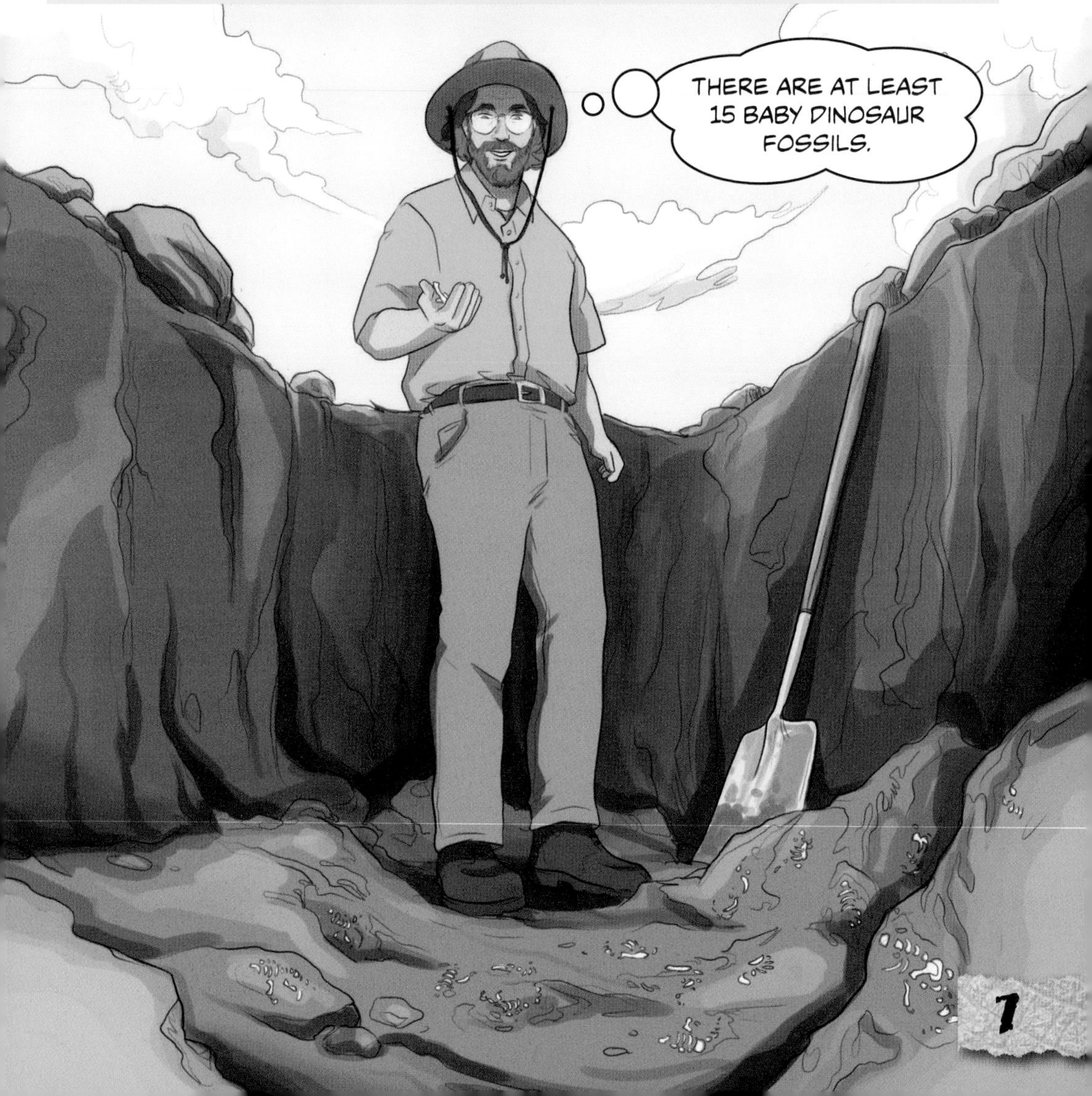
THERE ARE AT LEAST 15 BABY DINOSAUR FOSSILS.

CHAPTER 2

A NEST OF QUESTIONS

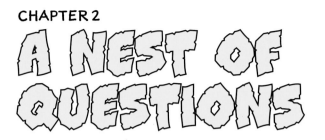

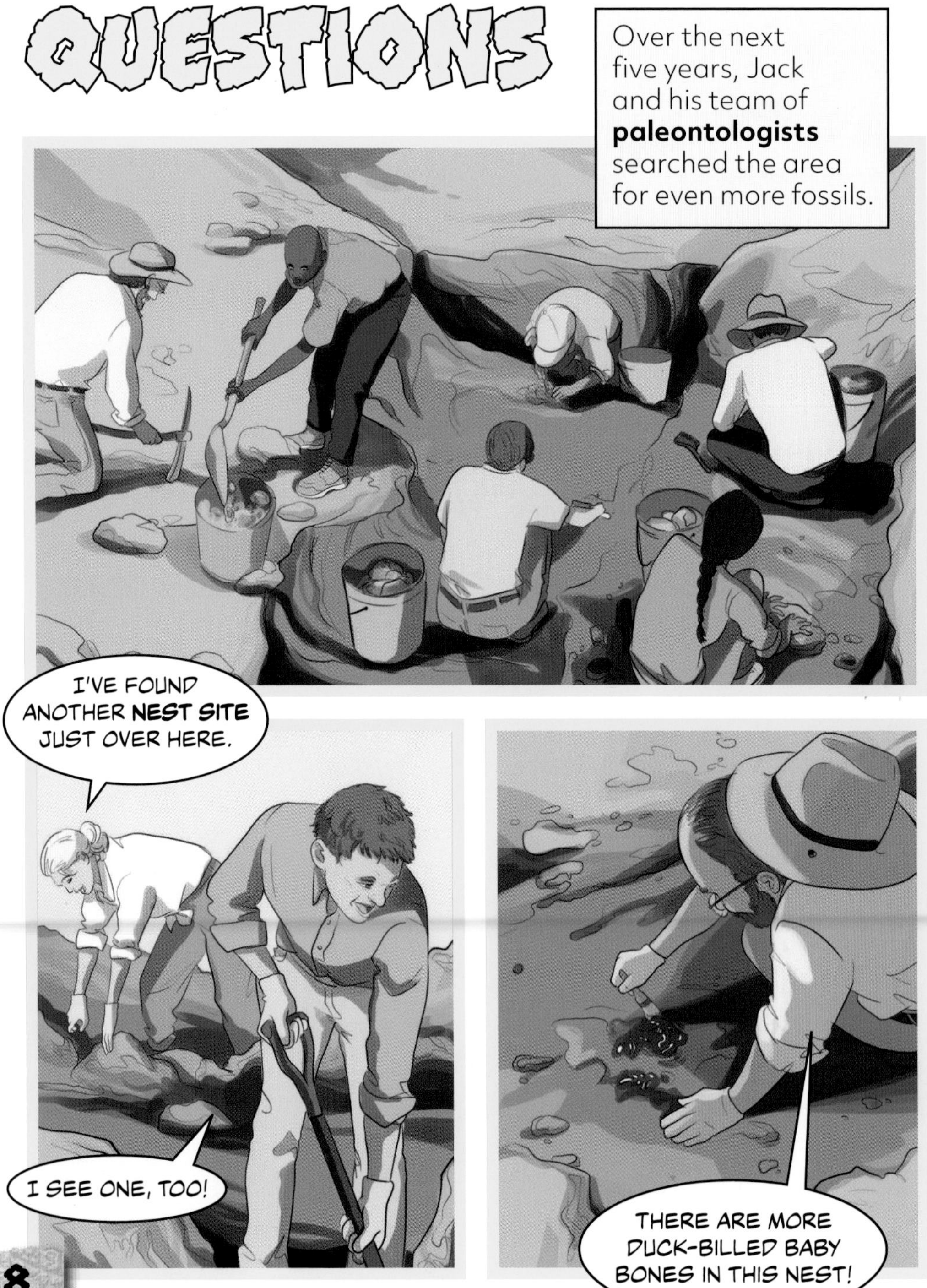
Over the next five years, Jack and his team of **paleontologists** searched the area for even more fossils.
I'VE FOUND ANOTHER **NEST SITE** JUST OVER HERE.
I SEE ONE, TOO!
THERE ARE MORE DUCK-BILLED BABY BONES IN THIS NEST!

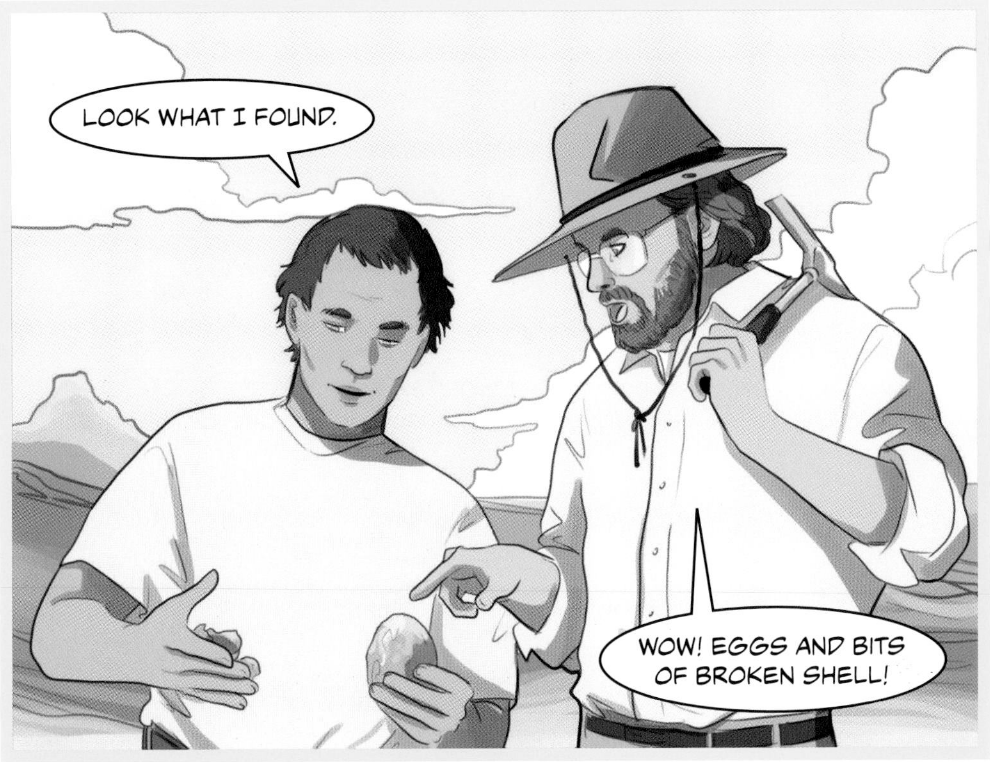
LOOK WHAT I FOUND.
WOW! EGGS AND BITS OF BROKEN SHELL!

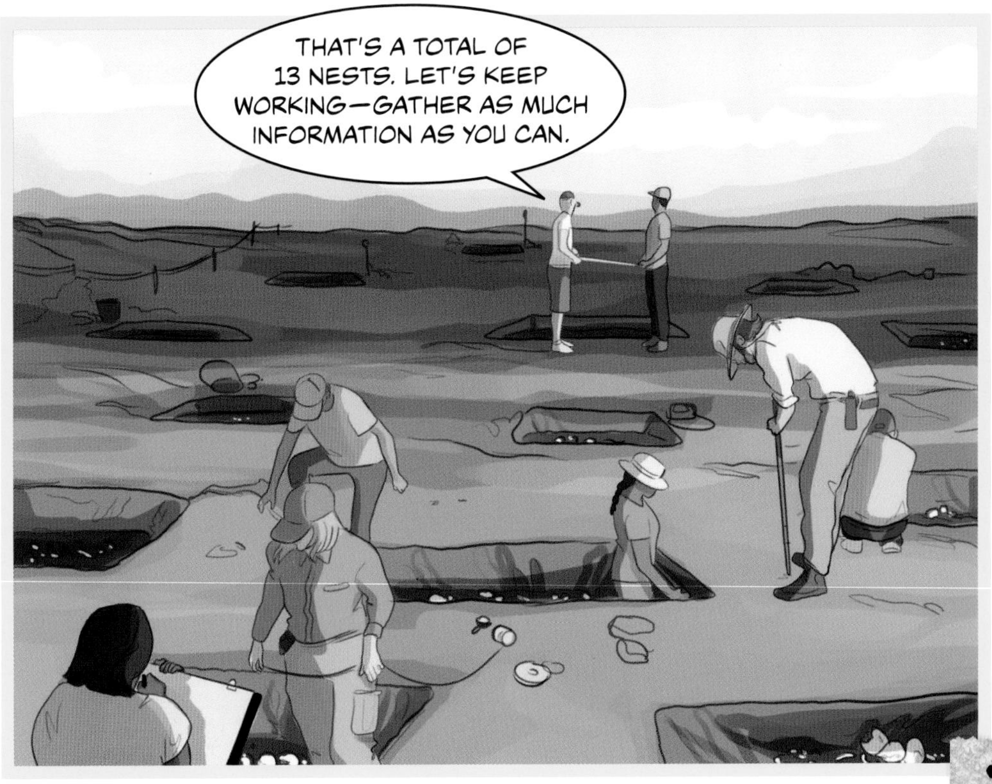
THAT'S A TOTAL OF 13 NESTS. LET'S KEEP WORKING—GATHER AS MUCH INFORMATION AS YOU CAN.

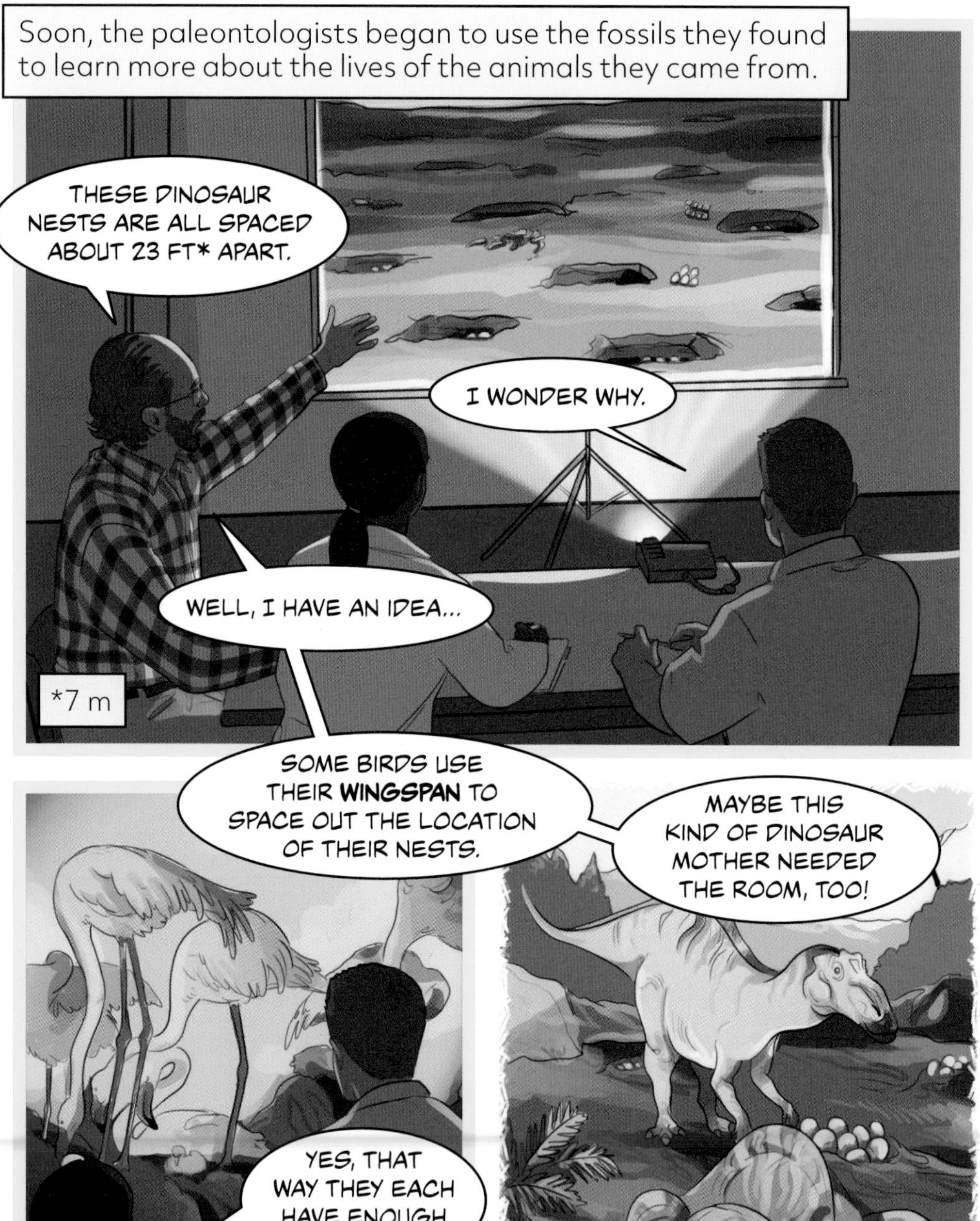

Soon, the paleontologists began to use the fossils they found to learn more about the lives of the animals they came from.
THESE DINOSAUR NESTS ARE ALL SPACED ABOUT 23 FT* APART.
I WONDER WHY.
WELL, I HAVE AN IDEA...
*7 m
SOME BIRDS USE THEIR **WINGSPAN** TO SPACE OUT THE LOCATION OF THEIR NESTS.
YES, THAT WAY THEY EACH HAVE ENOUGH ROOM.
MAYBE THIS KIND OF DINOSAUR MOTHER NEEDED THE ROOM, TOO!

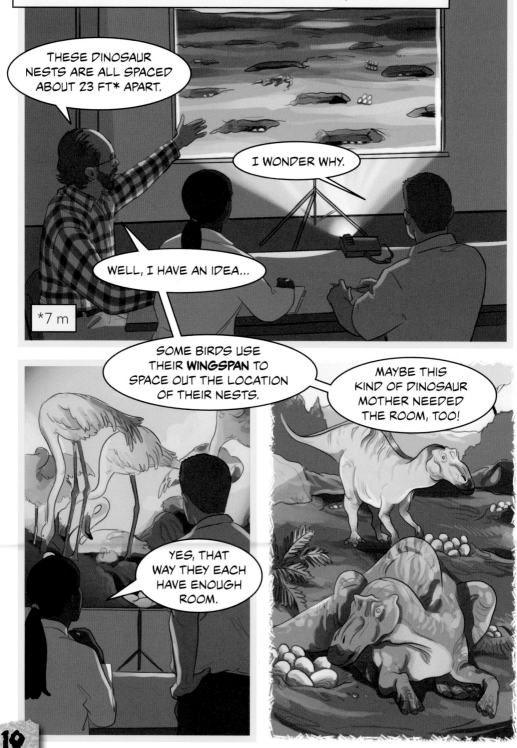

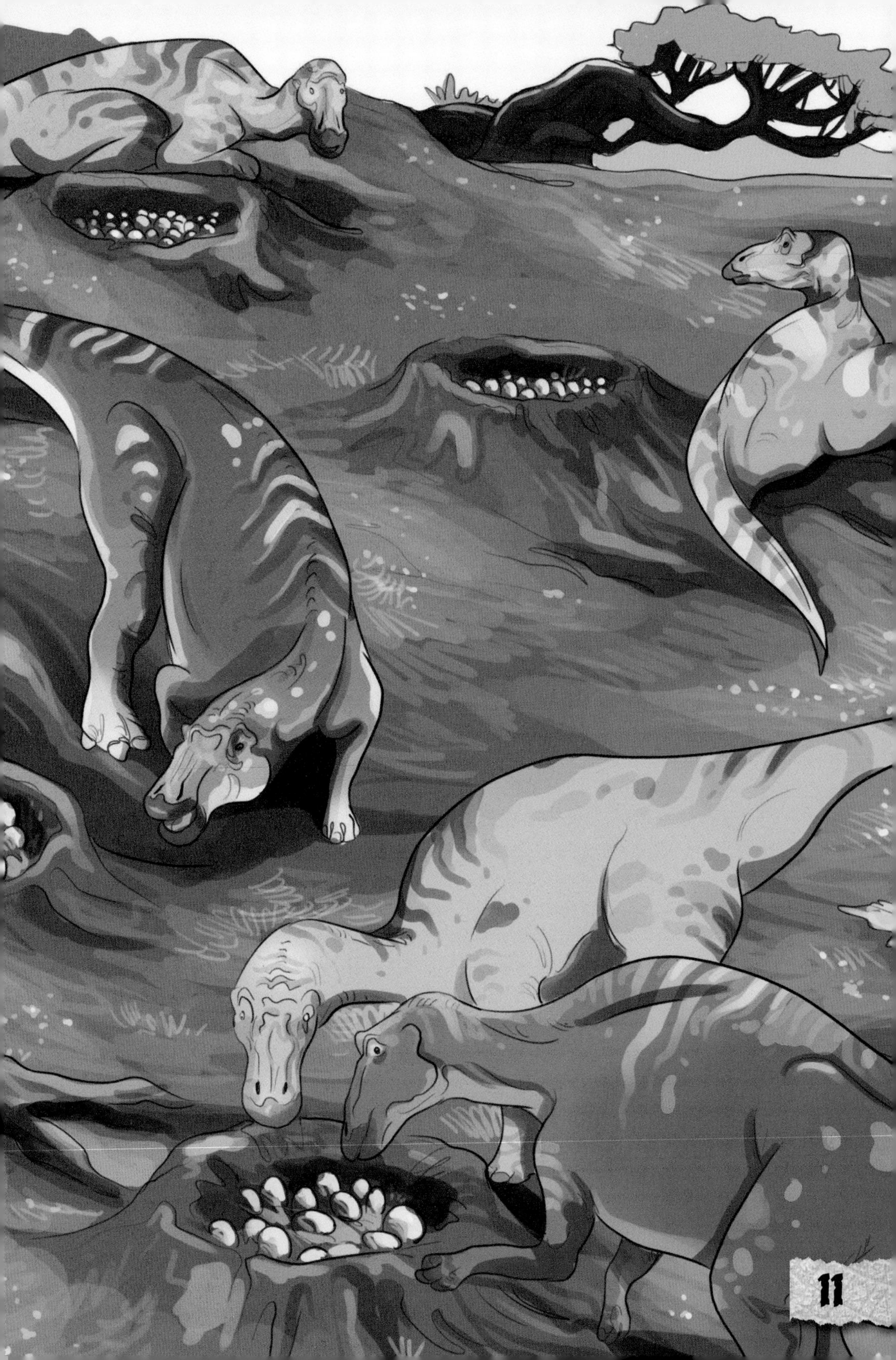

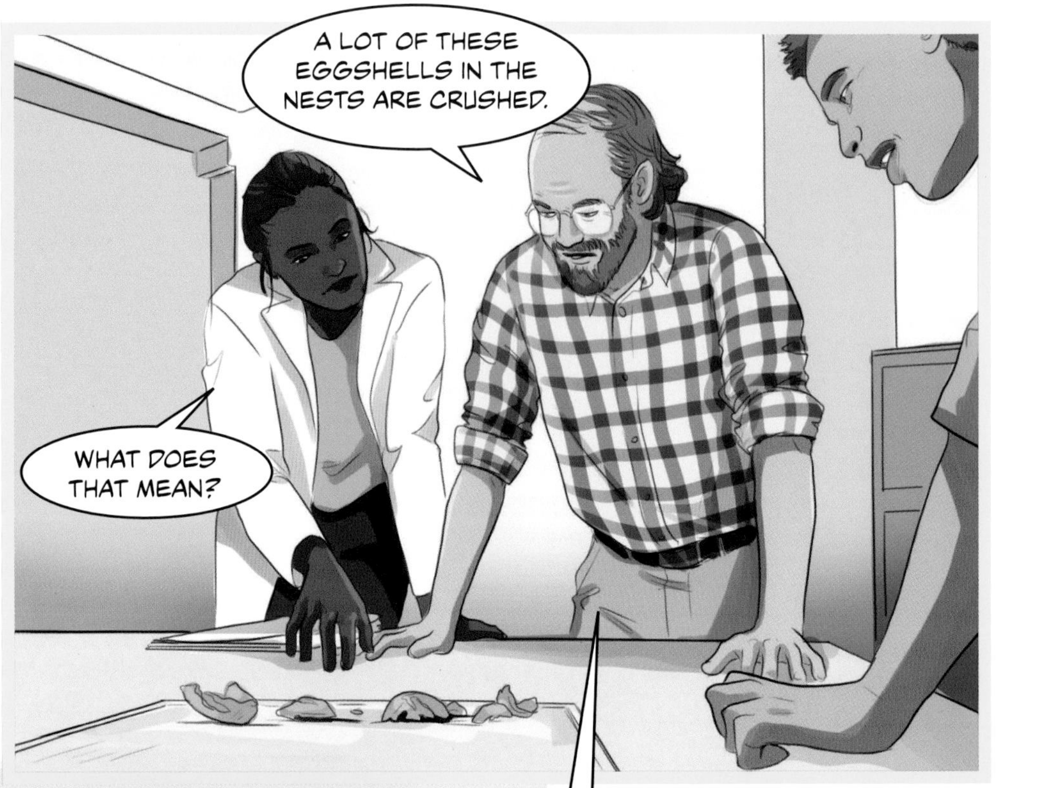
A LOT OF THESE EGGSHELLS IN THE NESTS ARE CRUSHED.
WHAT DOES THAT MEAN?

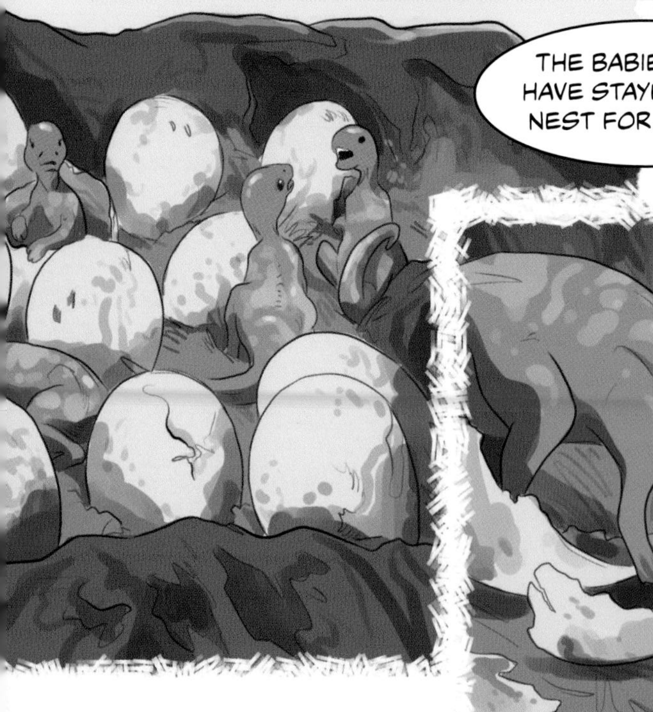
THE BABIES MUST HAVE STAYED IN THE NEST FOR A WHILE.

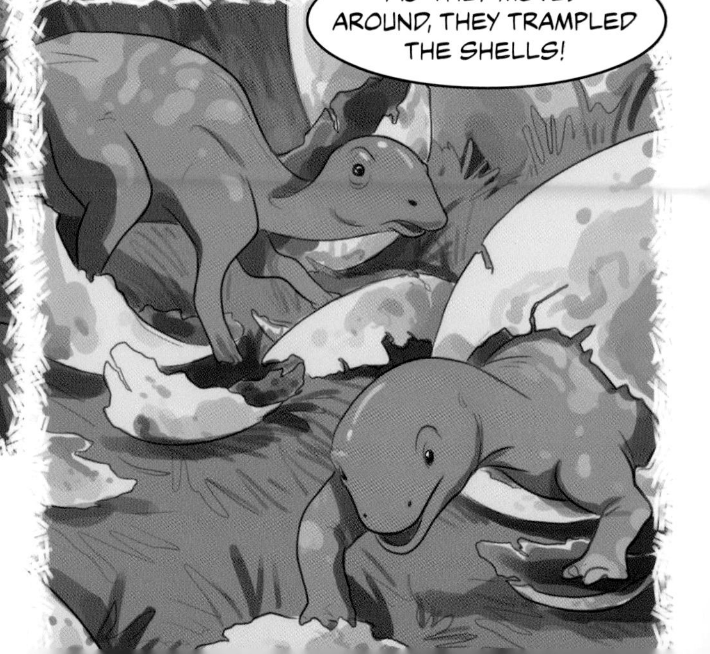
AS THEY MOVED AROUND, THEY TRAMPLED THE SHELLS!

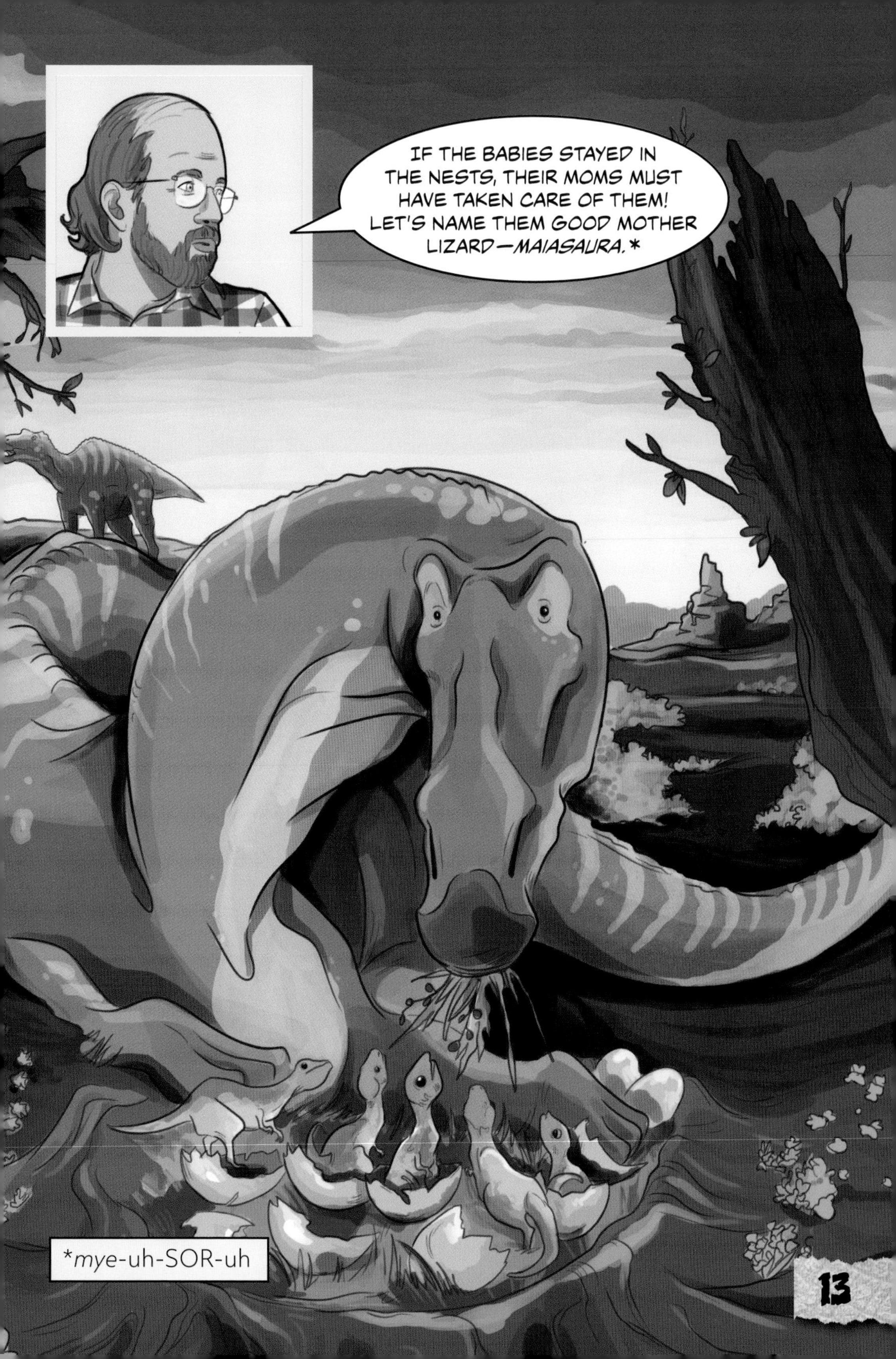
IF THE BABIES STAYED IN THE NESTS, THEIR MOMS MUST HAVE TAKEN CARE OF THEM! LET'S NAME THEM GOOD MOTHER LIZARD—*MAIASAURA.**
**mye*-uh-SOR-uh

CHAPTER 3

SOLVING PUZZLES

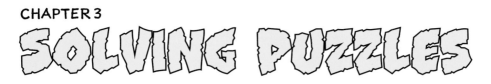

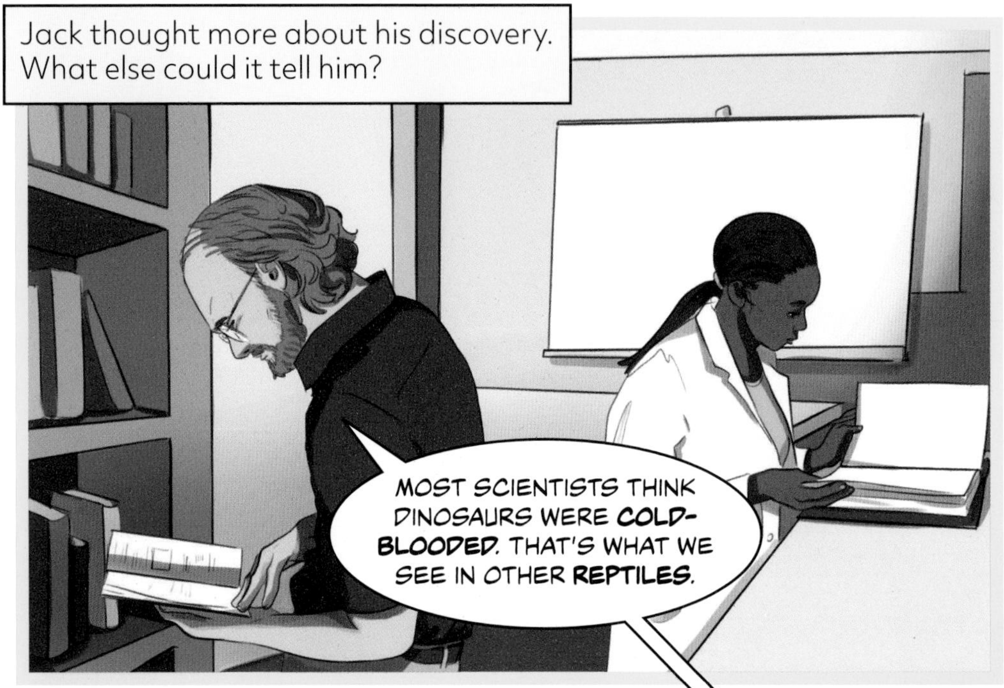
Jack thought more about his discovery. What else could it tell him?
MOST SCIENTISTS THINK DINOSAURS WERE **COLD-BLOODED**. THAT'S WHAT WE SEE IN OTHER **REPTILES**.

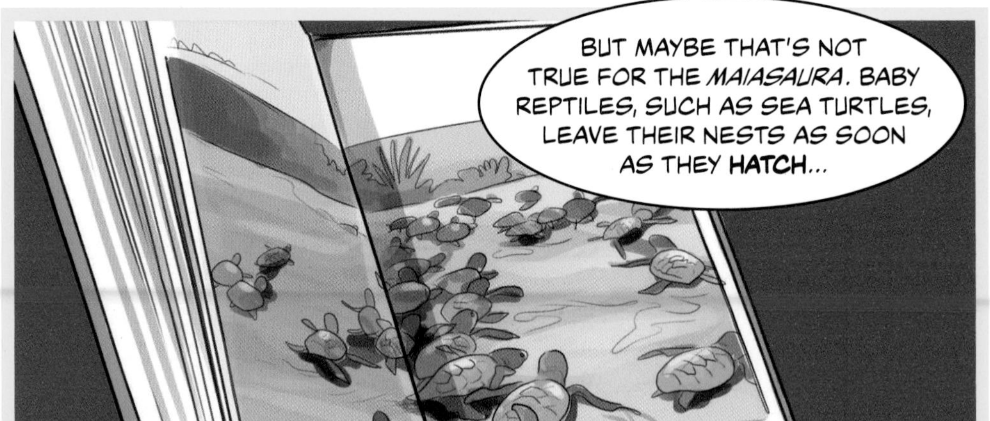
BUT MAYBE THAT'S NOT TRUE FOR THE *MAIASAURA*. BABY REPTILES, SUCH AS SEA TURTLES, LEAVE THEIR NESTS AS SOON AS THEY **HATCH**...

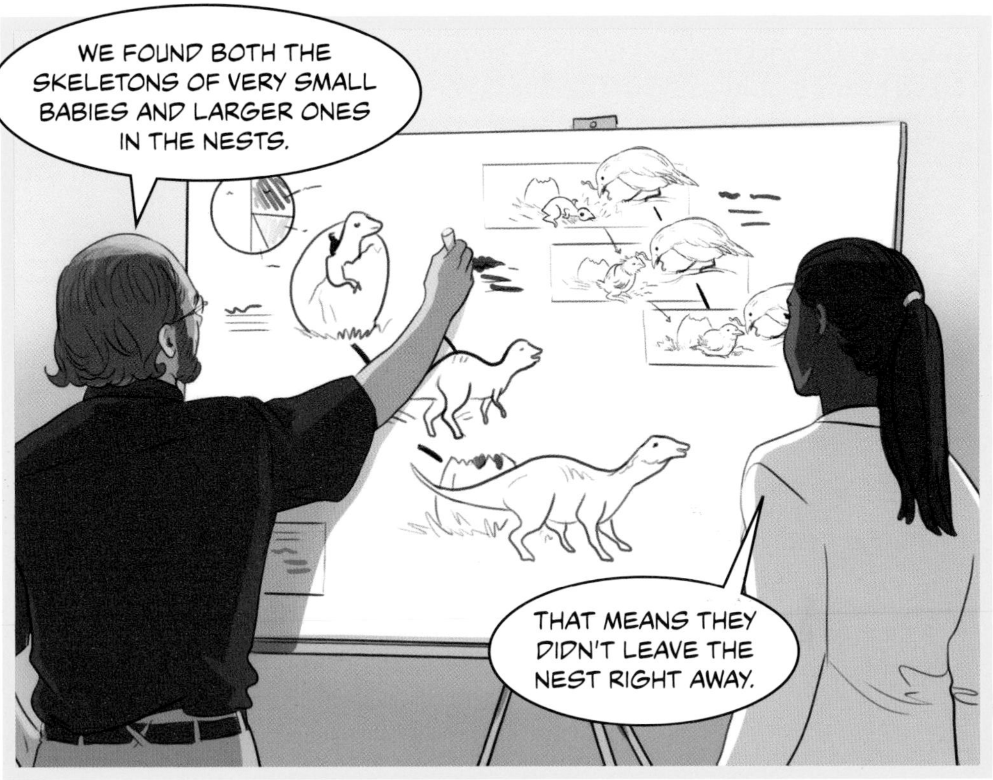
WE FOUND BOTH THE SKELETONS OF VERY SMALL BABIES AND LARGER ONES IN THE NESTS.
THAT MEANS THEY DIDN'T LEAVE THE NEST RIGHT AWAY.

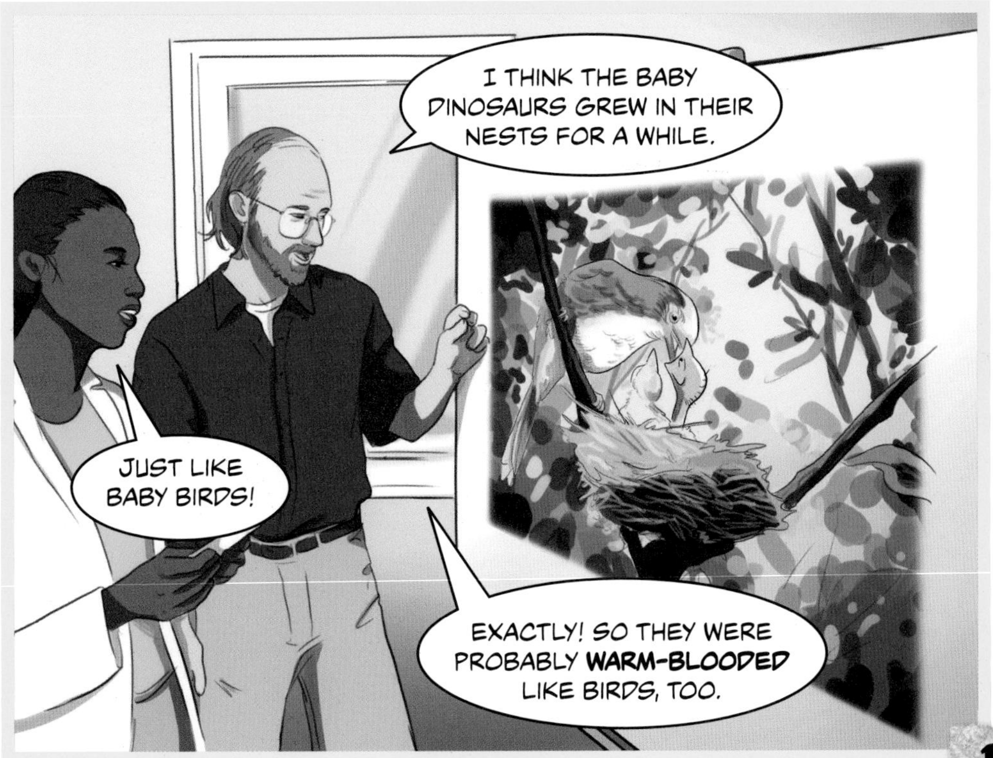
I THINK THE BABY DINOSAURS GREW IN THEIR NESTS FOR A WHILE.
JUST LIKE BABY BIRDS!
EXACTLY! SO THEY WERE PROBABLY **WARM-BLOODED** LIKE BIRDS, TOO.

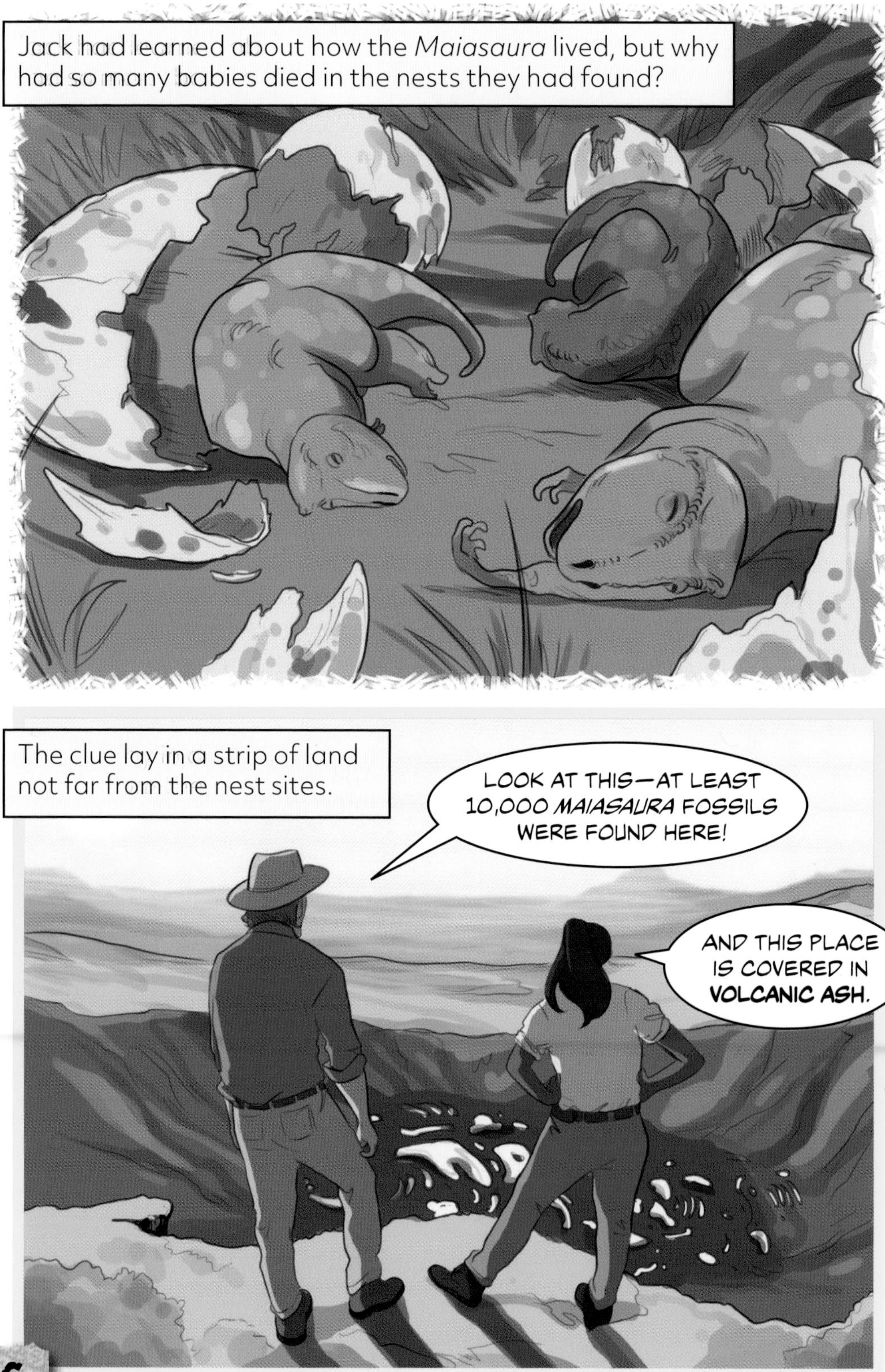
Jack had learned about how the *Maiasaura* lived, but why had so many babies died in the nests they had found?
The clue lay in a strip of land not far from the nest sites.
LOOK AT THIS—AT LEAST 10,000 *MAIASAURA* FOSSILS WERE FOUND HERE!
AND THIS PLACE IS COVERED IN **VOLCANIC ASH.**

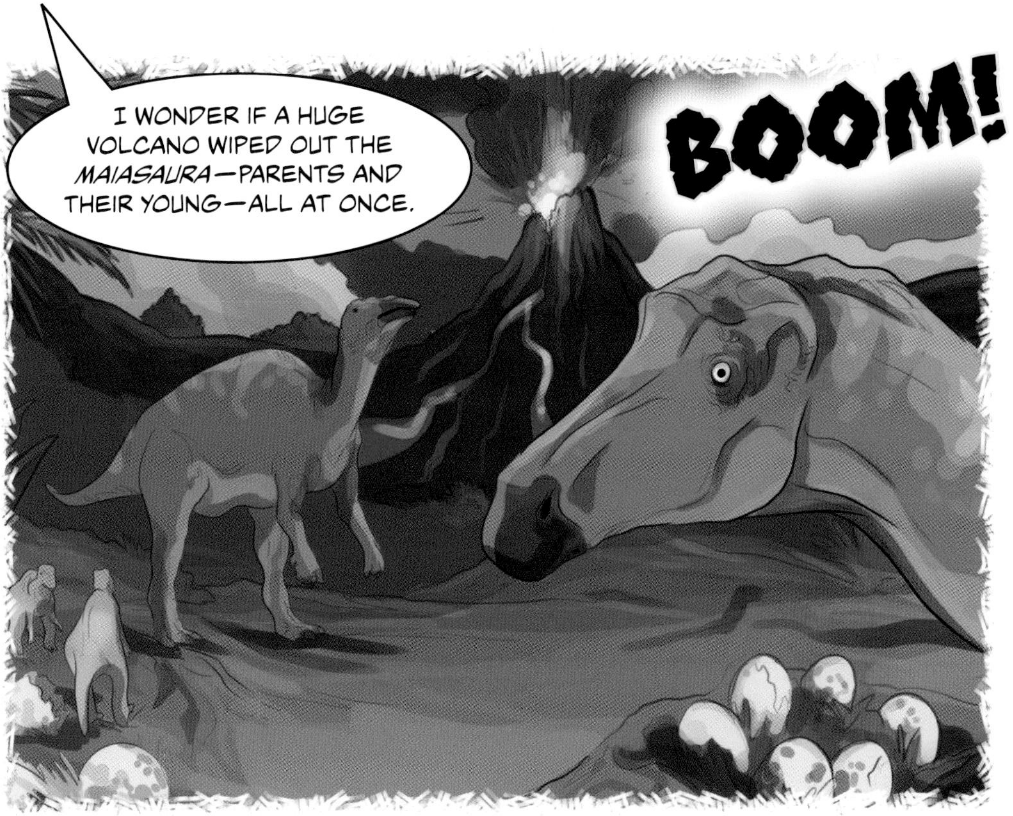
I WONDER IF A HUGE VOLCANO WIPED OUT THE *MAIASAURA*—PARENTS AND THEIR YOUNG—ALL AT ONCE.
BOOM!

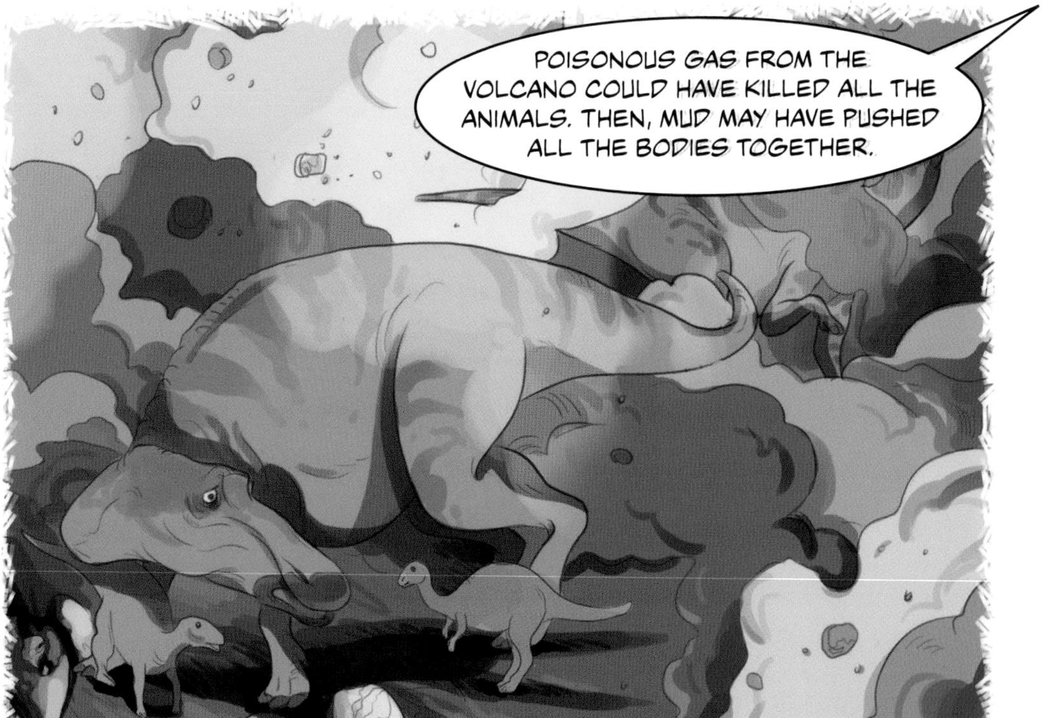
POISONOUS GAS FROM THE VOLCANO COULD HAVE KILLED ALL THE ANIMALS. THEN, MUD MAY HAVE PUSHED ALL THE BODIES TOGETHER.

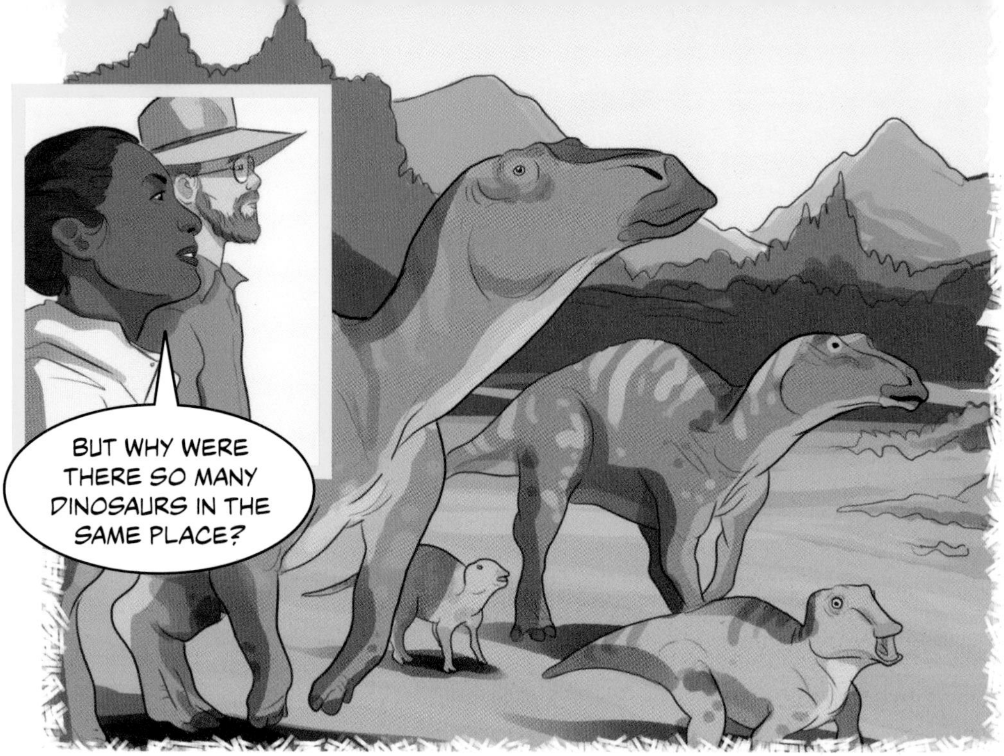
BUT WHY WERE THERE SO MANY DINOSAURS IN THE SAME PLACE?

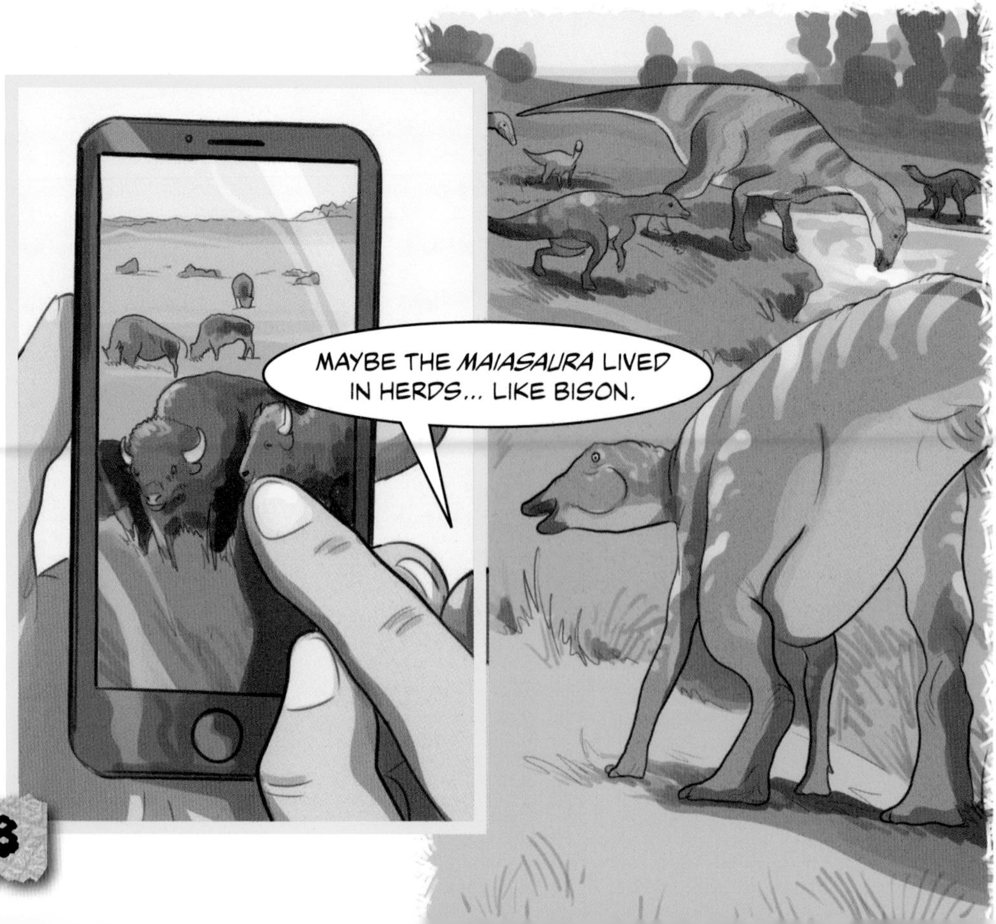
MAYBE THE *MAIASAURA* LIVED IN HERDS... LIKE BISON.

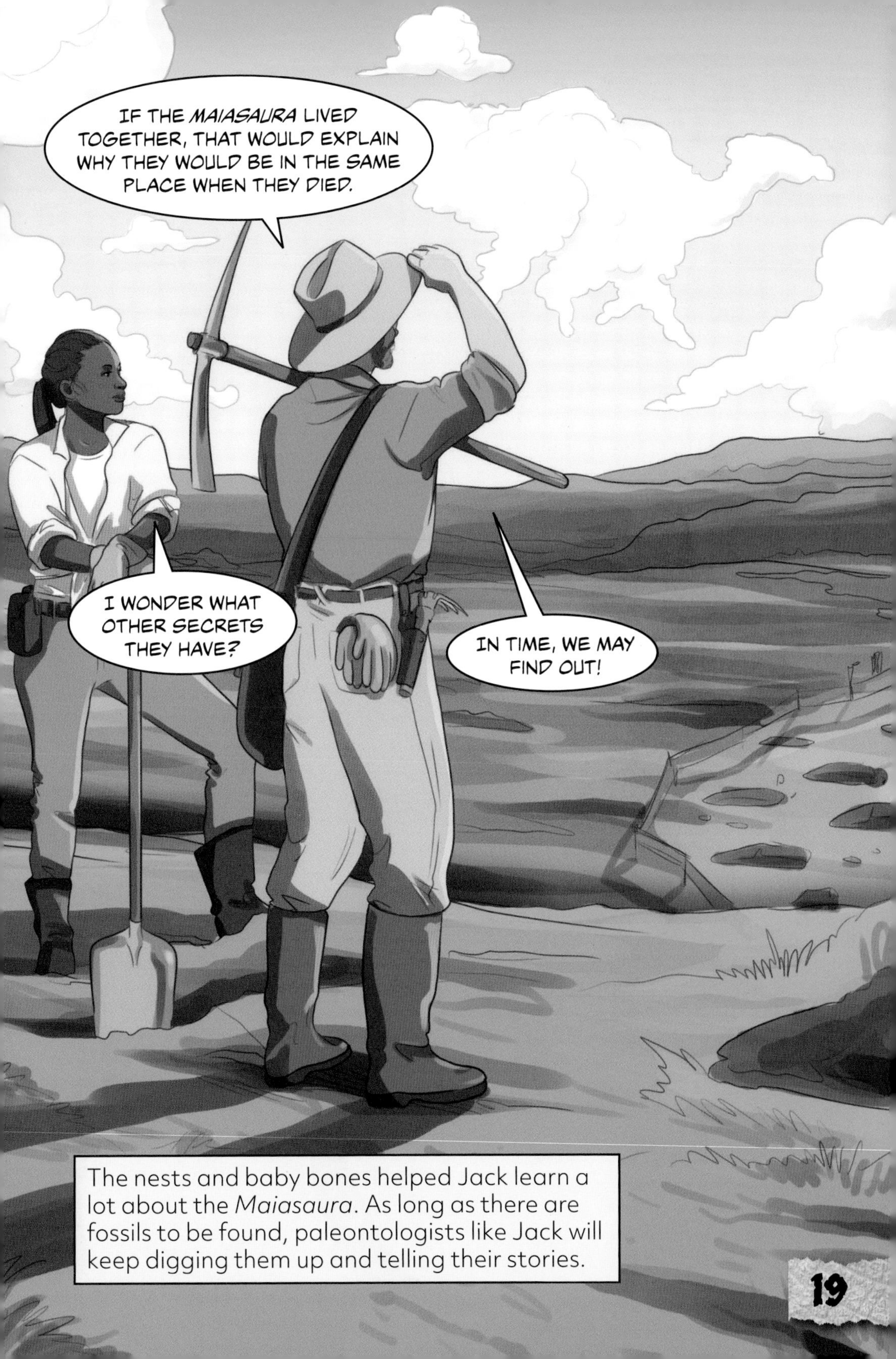
IF THE *MAIASAURA* LIVED TOGETHER, THAT WOULD EXPLAIN WHY THEY WOULD BE IN THE SAME PLACE WHEN THEY DIED.
I WONDER WHAT OTHER SECRETS THEY HAVE?
IN TIME, WE MAY FIND OUT!
The nests and baby bones helped Jack learn a lot about the *Maiasaura*. As long as there are fossils to be found, paleontologists like Jack will keep digging them up and telling their stories.

Who Lived with *Maiasaura*?

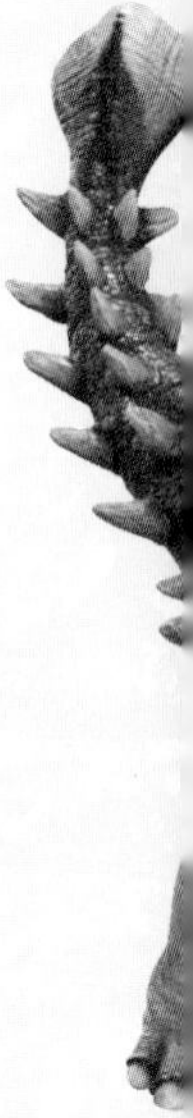

Dinosaurs lived on Earth for around 150 million years. Scientists divide the time in which the dinosaurs lived into three periods—the Triassic period (252 to 201 million years ago), the Jurassic period (201 to 145 million years ago), and the Cretaceous period (145 to 66 million years ago).

Maiasaura lived near the end of the Cretaceous period. Here are three other dinosaurs that lived at the same time and in the same place as *Maiasaura*.

ALBERTOSAURUS

(al-*bur*-toh-SOR-uhss)

This large, powerful meat-eater preyed on duck-billed dinosaurs. Here is what we know about the fierce predator.

- It walked on its two hind legs, using its long tail to help keep its balance.
- It had long jaws with about 70 large, saw-like teeth.
- It was 30 ft (9 m) long and 11 ft (3.4 m) high at the hips.

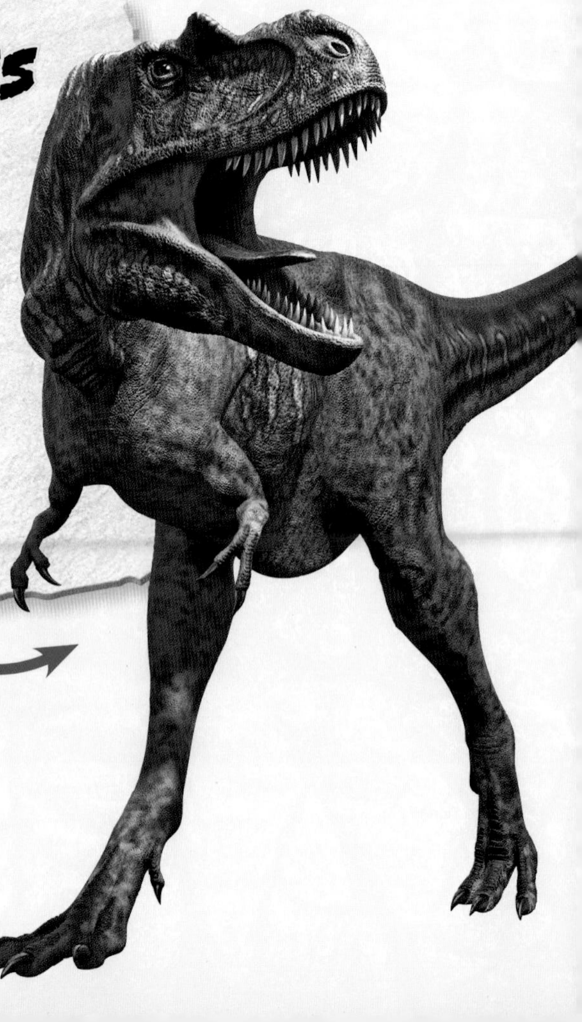

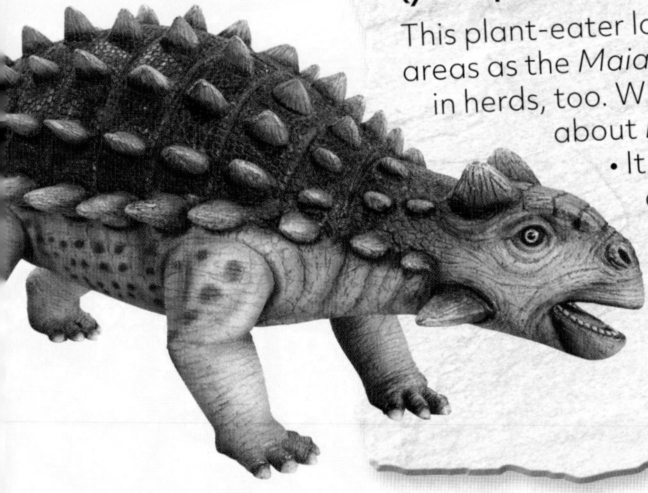

EUOPLOCEPHALUS

(yoo-op-luh-SEF-uh-luhss)

This plant-eater looked for food in the same areas as the *Maiasaura*. It probably traveled in herds, too. What else have we learned about *Euoplocephalus*?

- It belonged to a group of dinosaurs called ankylosaurs (AN-kee-luh-sorz).
- It had large horns and thick plates in its skin, which provided good protection from predators.
- It was 20 ft (6 m) long.

ORNITHOMIMUS

(or-*nith*-oh-MYE-muhss)

Ornithomimus probably ran in and out of the *Maiasaura* herds, searching for insects, fruit, eggs, and small reptiles to eat. What kind of creature was *Ornithomimus*?

- It looked similar to an ostrich, with a small head, long neck, and long legs.
- It could probably run as fast as 40 miles per hour (64 kph).
- It was 15–20 ft (4.5–6 m) long and 6–8 ft (1.8–2.4 m) high at the hips.

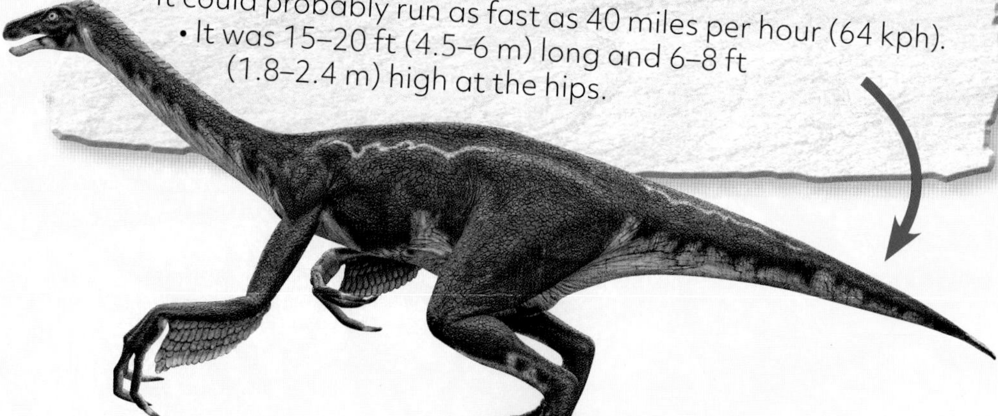

What Is Paleontology?

Paleontology is the study of fossils, which are what is left of things that lived millions of years ago. Fossils are found in rock. Paleontologists use special tools to carefully remove the fossils from the rock so they can study them. By studying fossils, paleontologists can figure out where a plant or animal lived, what it looked like, and how it lived.

SOMETIMES PALEONTOLOGISTS STUDY FOSSILS IN LABS. THERE, THEY CAN USE MORE TOOLS TO LEARN ABOUT ANCIENT PLANTS AND ANIMALS.

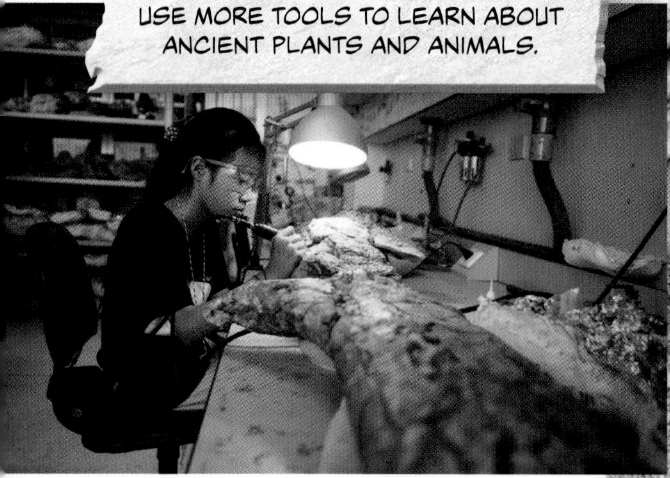

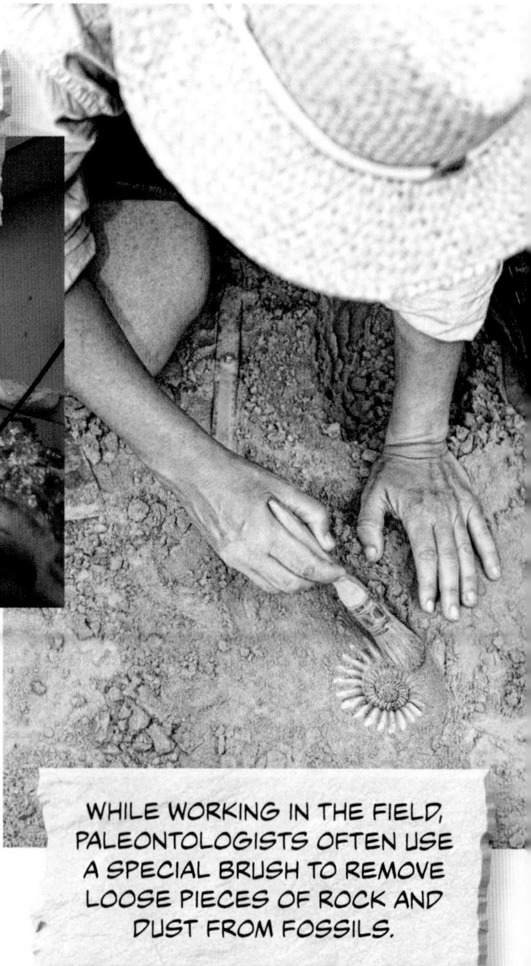

Fossils can show how living things changed over time, too. Paleontologists can use fossils to find out what happened to an **environment** in the past and how living things **adapted** to the changes.

WHILE WORKING IN THE FIELD, PALEONTOLOGISTS OFTEN USE A SPECIAL BRUSH TO REMOVE LOOSE PIECES OF ROCK AND DUST FROM FOSSILS.